Dinogirl

The Story of a Girl and a Dinosaur

By Denise Porcello

Illustrations by Clarissa Koos

Editorial Consultant Todd Civin

Copyright © Denise Porcello All Rights Reserved.

No part of this publication may be reproduced, stored in a retrieval system or transmitted in any form by any means electronic, mechanical, or photocopying, recording or otherwise without permission in writing from the author.

Request for permission to make copies of any part of the work should be submitted online to dinogirlbook@gmail.com

ISBN-10: 1514236052
ISBN-13: 978-1514236055

Printed in the United States
Amazon Create Space

This book is dedicated to Chip, who always supports my dreams; my daughters Casey and Samantha who are discovering their dreams; Michelle Cooke, Maureen Riordan, and Sherrie Ninteau, who inspired me to follow mine; the DIG School staff and to Clarissa and all girls who love science.

Denise Porcello

This book is dedicated to my Mom and Dad, who have supported me and helped make this all possible. I would also like to dedicate this to my friends, family, and teachers, both from here in California and at the dig site. To Denise Porcello for writing this amazing book that you're about to read. And lastly, to the dinosaurs that lived before us, for being so awesome!

Clarissa Koos

In memory of
Geoff Harrison
1954-2015

"Over here! Come look at this!" Clarissa, a 12-year-old girl from California, turned her head toward the voice. Geoff was pointing at a shape sticking out of the rock. Geoff Harrison was a paleontologist from the Burke Museum in Seattle, Washington.

A fossil is found in the rock.

A fossil!

"I told you that Montana was the place to be!"

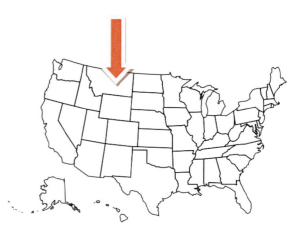

Layers of sedimentary rock hold fossils.

Clarissa couldn't believe her luck. Only a few months ago, her mother contacted Dr. Greg Wilson, a paleontologist from the University of Washington. A paleontologist is a person who studies fossils. Dr. Wilson invited Clarissa to go on a fossil dig.

Dr. Greg Wilson.

Clarissa thought back to the months leading up to the dig. All of her hard work was paying off. Clarissa liked discovering what a ==dinosaur== ate or how big it was by looking at fossils. She knew fossils were clues to the past. She also liked drawing dinosaurs.

Triceratops skull drawing by Clarissa.

Clarissa looked around at all of the excited faces. They got out their tools and got to work. Carefully, they picked away at the rock around the fossil. It was a bone – a dinosaur bone! And it was big!

Leg bone femur fossil.

As they uncovered the bone, they started to dig toward the left. Another bone! They were onto something big, something VERY big! Their excitement grew! It was hard to stop working at the end of each day.

Rib and leg bones were discovered.

Museum volunteer Wolf Gordon Clifton and Clarissa.

At the camp site, Clarissa and her museum friends would tell stories and watch the sunset.

On clear nights, Clarissa and her dad would use a telescope to look up into the starry Montana sky. With the telescope, they could see the moon and even Saturn with its many rings!

Montana's nickname is "Big Sky Country."

As the team worked, they found more bones: a rib, another leg bone. Then still more! Days went by, and still the team worked under the hot sun. Geoff brought in power tools to help break up the rock above and behind the fossils.

Breaking up rock with a jackhammer.

What kind of dinosaur was it? Geoff thought it might be a hadrosaur because of the tendon that was found. A hadrosaur was a large duck-billed dinosaur that lived approximately 65 million years ago. It had a big, thick tail and was an herbivore.

A tendon was uncovered near a leg bone.

"What will you name it?" Bruce Crowley asked Geoff. Geoff looked around at all of the excited faces. He smiled. "Clarissasaurus," he said.

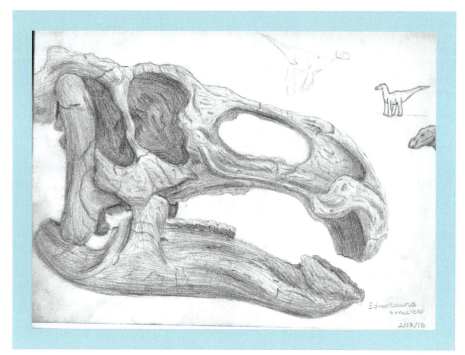

Edmontosaurus skull drawing by Clarissa.

Clarissa's face shone with pride. She sat down to sketch the bones in their exact positions. This would help the workers in the lab put the bones back together. She also sketched what the skull would look like.

Finally, the team had to stop for the season. The site was carefully covered with tarps to protect the bones for the long winter months. They had treated the bones with plaster and Vinac to help preserve them. Clarissa could not wait until next summer!

Vinac protects the fossils.

In the fall, Clarissa was back at school, busy with homework and piano and cello lessons. On weekends, she would visit museums and practice sketching the fossils she saw. She had loved dinosaurs since she was little and spent her free time learning as much as she could.

The next summer, Clarissasaurus was waiting for them when the team arrived. They got right to work.

Clarissa at the dig site, ready to work.

"You've gotten taller!" Geoff smiled at Clarissa. Clarissa smiled back and replied, "Stronger too! I have to help carry these back to the truck!"

After a few days, a team of teachers arrived from the DIG Field School to help. They took pictures of Clarissa.

DIG Field School teachers help prepare the fossils to be moved.

They wanted to hear her story. One teacher even wanted her autograph! Clarissa was embarrassed, but proud. The teachers got to work preparing the fossils to move.

"Hey Dinogirl!" Clarissa heard. When she looked up, she saw that the voice wasn't talking to her. The team was hugging Lauren Berg DeBey, a paleontologist from the University of Washington in Seattle, who had just arrived at the site.

Dr. DeBey arrives in the field.

Lauren looked over at Clarissa. "Great to have another Dinogirl here! Congratulations on Clarissasaurus!"

They covered the fossil bones with pads and then burlap strips covered in plaster. Some of the bones were so big, wooden boards were added to help protect Clarissasaurus.

Plaster and wood protect the bones for transport.

When one side of the bone was ready in its plaster cast, the team carefully removed the remaining rock.

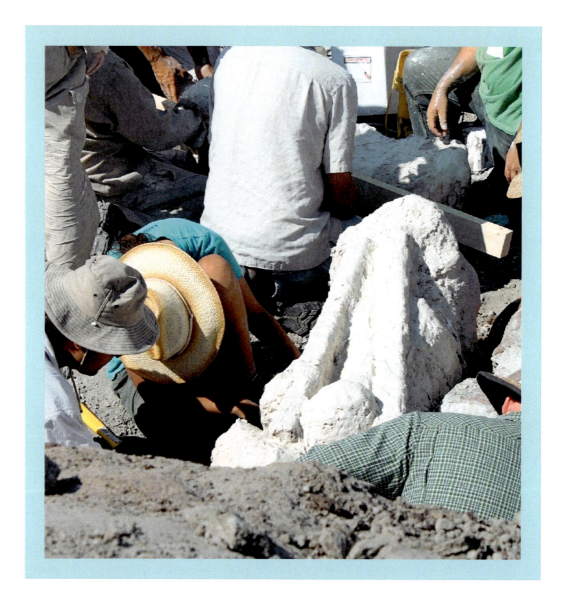

The remaining rock was chipped away.

Clarissa held her breath as the bone was rolled over. The plaster protected the bone until it could be brought back to the lab in Seattle. The bottom of the bone was covered the same way.

The fossils are ready to go to the lab.

"Rest up everyone!" Geoff called to the team. "Tomorrow we'll move them, and it's a long hike back to the truck!" "No problem," Clarissa smiled at him.

Heading back to the camp site.

It took six people to move each section of bone back to the truck. With all of the plaster and wood supports, the fossils weighed almost 700 pounds each! The last of the bones were loaded onto the truck. They were ready to go to the museum!

Wrapped fossils are ready to go to the laboratory.

"See you in a few months!" Geoff yelled to Clarissa. "Will you help us get the fossils ready at the museum?"

"I sure will!" Clarissa called back.

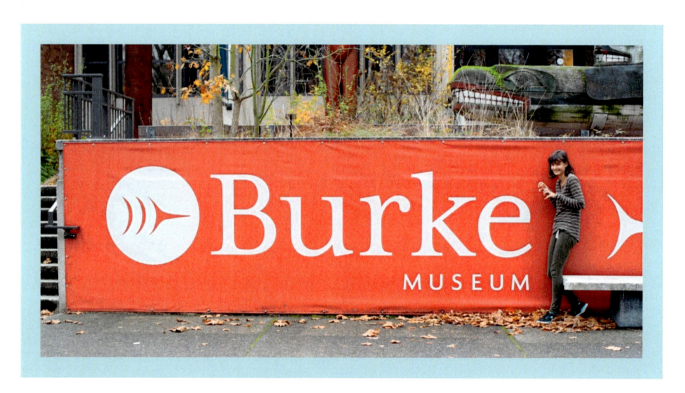

Clarissa arrives at the Burke Museum.

Back at the Burke Museum lab in Seattle, experts discovered the fossils were from an *Edmontosaurus*. An *Edmontosaurus* was an herbivore that lived during the Cretaceous period, about 66 million years ago. Its legs were 3 meters long! These bones were the second largest fossils to be found from this type of dinosaur!

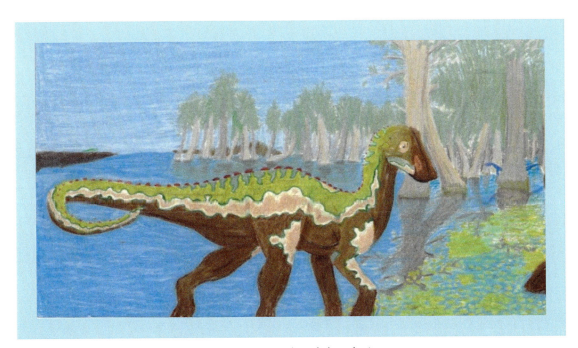

Edmontosaurus sketch by Clarissa.

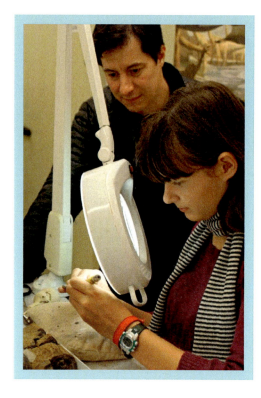

Clarissa helped to piece together the smaller parts.

It was like putting together a puzzle – a puzzle from the past.

Dr. Wilson and Clarissa put the small pieces together.

Working at the Burke Museum laboratory.

Being a Dinogirl was hard work, but there was nothing Clarissa would rather be!

Clarissa with the fossils from Clarissasuarus.

Glossary

Dinosaur – An animal that lived millions of years ago and is now extinct

Cretaceous period – Approximately 73 to 65 million years ago

Edmontosaurus – An herbivore that lived during the **Cretaceous** period, 66 million years ago

Extinct – Animals that are no longer alive and never will be

Fossil – Prints or remains of a plant or animal that have turned to stone

Hadrosaur – A duck-billed dinosaur that lived approximately 65 million years ago

Herbivore – An animal that eats plants

Museum – A place to go to study objects or artwork

Paleontologist – A person who studies fossils

Telescope – An instrument that makes far away objects look closer

Tendon – Tissue that attaches muscle to bone in the body

Vinac – A special clear liquid, like glue, that helps to protect fossils

Photo Credits

Geoff Harrison photo – Tom Wolken
Page 1 – Chuck Koos
Page 2 – Denise Porcello
Page 3 – Tom Wolken
Page 4 – Clarissa Koos
Page 5 – Denise Porcello
Page 6 – Chuck Koos
Page 7 – Tom Wolken
Page 8 – Chuck Koos
Page 9 – Liz Koos
Page 10 – Clarissa Koos
Page 11 – Liz Koos
Page 12 – Tom Wolken
Page 13 – Liz Koos
Page 14 – Winifred Kehl
Page 15 – Liz Koos
Page 16 – Denise Porcello
Page 17 – Denise Porcello
Page 18 – Tom Wolken
Page 19 – Denise Porcello
Page 20 – Tom Wolken
Page 21 – Clarissa Koos
Page 22 – Tom Wolken
Page 23 – Tom Wolken
Page 24 – Tom Wolken
Page 27 – Tom Wolken
Page 28 – Lauren Berg DeBey
Little dino logo – Clarissa Koos and Lily Stokes

About Clarissa

Clarissa lives in coastal southern California. Her interest in dinosaurs started at a young age while playing with dinosaur toys and reading dinosaur books; her passion keeps growing as the years go on. Clarissa considers her "home away from home" to be the Natural History Museum of Los Angeles, where she likes to spend time drawing fossils. Her favorite subjects at school are science, art, and orchestra. Her hobbies include playing piano and cello, drawing, arts/crafts, reading, and playing with her two golden retrievers, Mario and Luigi. Clarissa's dream is to be a paleontologist. She hopes this book inspires other girls to follow their dreams in science!

Clarissa's family, friends, schoolmates, and teachers have all been supportive in her paleontological interests. She'd like to thank them for putting up with her endless dinosaur lectures! She would also like to thank Kathy Hall, Greg Wilson, Geoff Harrison, and Denise Porcello for making all of this possible. A special thanks to Luis Chiappe and Maureen Walsh at the Natural History Museum of Los Angeles.

DIG Field School

The Next Generation Science Standards state that "K-12 science education should reflect the interconnected nature of science as it is practiced and experienced in the real world." The Discoveries in Geosciences (DIG) Field School connects K-12 teachers with real scientists from the University of Washington and the Burke Museum. Teachers and paleontologists work side by side to investigate the extinction of dinosaurs and the rise of mammals at an active research site in Montana.

DIG Field School is free for teachers and includes four days at an active paleontological field research site; Continuing Education Units for participants; lesson plans and course materials; and ongoing educational coaching.

Learn more about the DIG Field School experience or how to apply by visiting http://digfieldschool.org. All proceeds from this book will support the DIG Field School.

Made in the USA
San Bernardino, CA
13 August 2015